holiday
cooking

Chef
express

Published by:
TRIDENT REFERENCE PUBLISHING
801 12th Avenue South, Suite 400
Naples, Fl 34102 USA

Tel: + 1 (239) 649-7077
www.tridentreference.com
email: sales@tridentreference.com

Holiday Cooking
© TRIDENT REFERENCE PUBLISHING

Publisher
Simon St. John Bailey

Editor-in-chief
Susan Knightley

Prepress
Precision Prep & Press

Includes Index
ISBN 1582796785
UPC 6 15269 96785 0

Printed in The United States

introduction

Choosing the menu is part of the excitement in the lead-up to a holiday celebration. Will it be the traditional roast turkey, ham, lamb or beef, or are you seeking for a different option? Whatever your preference, you're sure to find it here.

holiday cooking
introduction

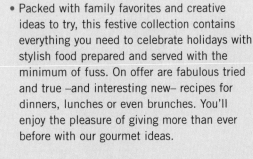

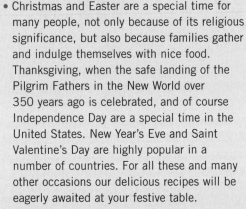

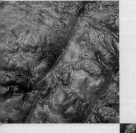

- Packed with family favorites and creative
  ideas to try, this festive collection contains
  everything you need to celebrate holidays with
  stylish food prepared and served with the
  minimum of fuss. On offer are fabulous tried
  and true –and interesting new– recipes for
  dinners, lunches or even brunches. You'll
  enjoy the pleasure of giving more than ever
  before with our gourmet ideas.

- Christmas and Easter are a special time for
  many people, not only because of its religious
  significance, but also because families gather
  and indulge themselves with nice food.
  Thanksgiving, when the safe landing of the
  Pilgrim Fathers in the New World over
  350 years ago is celebrated, and of course
  Independence Day are a special time in the
  United States. New Year's Eve and Saint
  Valentine's Day are highly popular in a
  number of countries. For all these and many
  other occasions our delicious recipes will be
  eagerly awaited at your festive table.

- Inviting family and friends to brunch over the holidays is an easy and relaxed way to entertain. Our salad recipes make ideal starters or main meals on their own. They are ideal for using up any leftovers such as jam and turkey, and make perfect brunch fare.

- As a stunning dessert is the perfect finale to any holiday meal, we have gathered our most requested sweet treats at the end of this book. And, as some of the nicest presents people can give at holidays are those that are homemade, and gifts of food are specially welcome, we provide you with fruit cake and pudding recipes that make delightful presents for family and friends. Wrap them in cellophane or pack them in boxes or baskets and use ribbons, baubles and tinsel to give your gifts that festive touch.

Difficulty scale

■□□I Easy to do

■■□I Requires attention

■■■I Requires experience

smoked
turkey salad

■□□ | Cooking time: 0 minute - Preparation time: 5 minutes

method

1. Wash and crisp salad greens. Slice turkey.
2. Arrange greens on serving plates and top with turkey, tomatoes and pecans.
3. To make vinaigrette, whisk together mustard, vinegar, garlic and cranberries, gradually adding oil, until combined and slightly thickened. Season to taste with salt and black pepper. Drizzle over salads.

....

Serves 6

ingredients

> assorted salad greens
> 750 g/1 1/2 lb smoked turkey
> 300 g/9 1/2 oz cherry tomatoes
> 90 g/3 oz pecans, toasted

cranberry vinaigrette

> 1 teaspoon wholegrain mustard
> 1 tablespoon balsamic vinegar
> 1 clove garlic, finely chopped
> 2 tablespoons canned, preserved cranberries
> 125 ml/4 fl oz olive oil
> salt and freshly ground black pepper

tip from the chef

To enrich the salad, you can use Parmesan cheese shavings (or feta cheese cubes) and croûtons.

prawn
and melon salad

■■□ | Cooking time: 0 minute - Preparation time: 15 minutes

ingredients

> **1 kg/2 lb cooked large prawns**
> **2 red apples**
> **2 tablespoons lime juice**
> **1 small rockmelon**
> **1 green pepper**
> **3 stalks celery**

island dressing

> **$^1/_2$ cup mayonnaise**
> **$^1/_4$ cup tomato sauce**
> **1 teaspoon Dijon mustard**
> **1 teaspoon Worcestershire sauce**

method

1. Peel prawns, leaving tail intact, remove back vein. Cut apples into slices, toss in lime juice. Peel rockmelon, cut into cubes. Seed green pepper, cut into cubes. Slice celery.
2. To make dressing, place mayonnaise, tomato sauce, Dijon mustard and Worcestershire sauce in a small bowl, stir to mix well.
3. Combine prawns, apples, rockmelon, green pepper and celery in a serving bowl, pour over dressing. Garnish with extra prawns, if desired.

....
Serves 8

tip from the chef

This salad is also exquisite if avocado is used instead of apple.

chicken
and veal terrine

■□□ I Cooking time: 90 minutes - Preparation time: 10 minutes

method

1. Remove rind from bacon. Arrange bay leaves in a decorative pattern on base of a loaf pan. Line base and sides of pan with bacon (a), leaving enough for the top.
2. Combine chicken, pork and veal mince with garlic, onions, pine nuts, egg, brandy, basil and parsley (b). Season to taste with salt and pepper. Press firmly into loaf pan (c). Top with remaining bacon.
3. Cover pan with foil, bake in moderate oven for 1¹/₂ hours, allow to cool, refrigerate overnight. Serve sliced.

....
Serves 8

ingredients

> **250 g/¹/₂ lb bacon slices**
> **4 bay leaves**
> **375 g/³/₄ lb chicken mince**
> **375 g/³/₄ lb pork and veal mince**
> **2 cloves garlic, crushed**
> **2 onions, very finely chopped**
> **¹/₃ cup pine nuts**
> **1 egg, lightly beaten**
> **2 tablespoons brandy**
> **1 tablespoon chopped basil**
> **1 tablespoon chopped parsley**
> **salt and freshly ground black pepper**

tip from the chef

As an option with less fat, replace bacon for briefly blanched spinach leaves.

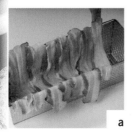

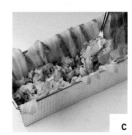

a   b   c

ham salad
with mustard dressing

■□□ | Cooking time: 0 minute - Preparation time: 10 minutes

ingredients

> **1 mignonette lettuce**
> **500 g/1 lb cooked ham**
> **250 g/¹/₂ lb cheese
  of your choice**
> **4 sticks celery**
> **4 gherkins**
> **250 g/¹/₂ lb cherry
  tomatoes**

dressing

> **¹/₂ cup mayonnaise**
> **¹/₄ cup yogurt**
> **2 teaspoons Dijon
  mustard**
> **2 teaspoons chopped
  fresh dill**

method

1. Separate leaves from lettuce. Cut ham into bite-sized pieces. Cut cheese into cubes. Slice celery and gherkins.
2. Line a salad plate with lettuce leaves. Arrange ham, cheese, celery, gherkins and tomatoes over lettuce.
3. To make dressing combine mayonnaise, yogurt, mustard and dill. Drizzle over salad.

....
Serves 6

tip from the chef
*This recipe is ideal to use up ham leftovers.
If you don't have the indicated amount,
complete with grilled chicken strips.*

sauces
for meats or poultry

■□□ | Cooking time: 3-6 minutes - Preparation time: 10 minutes

method

1. To make cranberry sauce place all ingredients in a small saucepan over medium heat. Stir until mixture boils, simmer for 1 minute. Pour into a hot sterilized jar, label and seal. Store in the refrigerator. Serve with turkey or other poultry.
2. To make cumberland sauce melt jelly in a small saucepan over low heat. Stir in marmalade, juices and port. Simmer for 1 minute. Remove from heat and cool. Store in an airtight container in the refrigerator. Serve with pork or ham.
3. To make apple sauce place apples and water in a small saucepan with a tight-fitting lid. Bring to the boil, cover and simmer for 5 minutes or until apples are very soft. Remove from heat and beat in remaining ingredients. Spoon into hot sterilized jars, label and seal. Store in the refrigerator. Serve with pork or duck.

ingredients

spicy cranberry sauce

> 1 cup canned or bottled cranberry sauce
> 1 teaspoon finely chopped fresh ginger
> 1 teaspoon ground cardamom
> 1/2 teaspoon cinnamon
> 2 teaspoons Worcestershire sauce

cumberland sauce

> 4 tablespoons redcurrant jelly
> 1 tablespoon citrus marmalade
> juice of 1 orange and 1/2 lemon
> 1/3 cup port

honey apple sauce

> 3 Granny Smith apples, peeled and diced
> 2 tablespoons water
> 2 tablespoons honey
> 2 teaspoons butter
> 1 teaspoon grated lemon rind
> pinch of ground cloves

tip from the chef

Cumberland sauce results delicious if a handful of fresh raspberries is added one minute before removing from heat.

potato
cake stacks with tuna

■ ■ □ | Cooking time: 35 minutes - Preparation time: 15 minutes

method

1. Preheat oven to 160°C/325°F/Gas 3. Pour stock into a baking dish just large enough to hold fish. Place fish in dish, cover with foil and bake, basting every 15 minutes, for 30-35 minutes or until cooked.
2. Lift salmon from dish, cool slightly and remove the skin, leaving head and tail intact. Place on a serving plate, cover loosely with plastic food wrap and chill.
3. To make aioli, stir garlic into mayonnaise. To make mango sauce, purée mango slices in a food processor with vinegar and mint. Gradually whisk in oil. To make remoulade, fold capers and gherkins into mayonnaise, stir in mustard and parsley. Chill sauces until ready to serve.
4. Toss red and green peppers with little vinaigrette. Spoon along length of fish. Serve fish at room temperature with sauces.

Serves 8-10

ingredients

> 750 ml/1¼ pt fish stock
> 1 x 1.5 kg/3 lb whole fresh salmon
> red and green peppers, cut into thin strips
> bottled or homemade vinaigrette

aioli

> 2 cloves garlic, finely chopped
> 250 g/8 oz mayonnaise

mango mint sauce

> 220 g/7 oz canned mango slices, drained
> 1 tablespoon white wine vinegar
> 1 tablespoon chopped fresh mint
> 2 tablespoons olive oil

remoulade

> 1 tablespoon capers
> 1 tablespoon finely chopped gherkins
> 250 g/8 oz mayonnaise
> 2 tablespoons Dijon mustard
> 1 tablespoon chopped fresh parsley

tip from the chef

Serve this special fish dish with boiled new potatoes and a tossed green salad.

chicken galantine
with citrus sauce

french
stuffed turkey

■ ■ ■ | Cooking time: 4 hours - Preparation time: 20 minutes

method

1. To make each stuffing, combine all ingredients and season to taste.
2. Preheat oven to 180°C/350°F/Gas 4. Carefully loosen skin from neck and breast of turkey and loosely fill with forcemeat stuffing. Press outside of breast to mold into shape, secure neck skin to back with skewers and tuck wings under body.
3. Spoon bread stuffing into turkey cavity. Secure opening and tie legs close to body with string. Wipe bird dry, spread with butter and season to taste with salt and black pepper.
4. Place turkey on a rack in a baking dish, add stock, cover dish tightly with foil and roast, basting every 20-25 minutes, for 3 1/2-4 hours or until juices run clear when thigh is pierced with a skewer. Remove foil for the last 30 minutes of cooking to allow turkey to brown. Transfer turkey to a heated platter, cover and stand for 15 minutes before carving.

Serves 8-10

ingredients

> 1 x 6 kg/12 lb turkey
> 60 g/2 oz butter, softened
> salt and freshly ground black pepper
> 500 ml/16 fl oz turkey stock

forcemeat stuffing

> 375 g/12 oz each lean pork and veal mince
> 90 g/3 oz breadcrumbs
> 1 tablespoon chopped mixed herbs
> 2 onions, chopped
> 60 g/ 2 oz bacon, chopped
> 1 egg, beaten
> 90 g/3 oz pecans, toasted and chopped
> 1 teaspoon grated lemon rind

bread stuffing

> 8 spring onions, finely chopped
> 30 g/1 oz butter
> 125 g/4 oz breadcrumbs
> 2 tablespoon snipped fresh chives
> 1 tablespoon chopped mixed herbs
> 1 teaspoon grated lemon rind
> 1 egg, beaten

tip from the chef

The turkey can be brushed with honey some minutes before taking away from the oven. Serve with apple purée.

duck a l'orange

■ ■ □ | Cooking time: 90 minutes - Preparation time: 20 minutes

ingredients

> 2 x 2.5 kg/5 lb ducks
> rind of 1 orange
> salt and freshly ground black pepper

orange sauce

> 4 tablespoons sugar
> 60 ml/2 fl oz vinegar
> 375 ml/12 fl oz duck stock
> 1 1/2 tablespoons cornflour blended with 2 tablespoons port
> rind of 2 oranges, shredded
> 125 ml/4 fl oz port
> 2 tablespoons orange-flavored liqueur
> 1 tablespoon butter

method

1. Preheat oven to 220°C/425°F/Gas 7. Remove excess fat from ducks, place orange rind into cavities and season to taste. Truss and place, breast-side-up, in a baking dish.
2. Bake for 20 minutes or until ducks brown and release some fat. Pour off fat. Reduce oven temperature to 190°C/375°F/Gas 5 and roast for 1 hour or until cooked.
3. To make sauce, stir sugar and vinegar in a saucepan over high heat to make a thick syrup. Remove from heat and gradually stir in stock. Return to heat and bring to the boil. Add cornflour mixture and orange rind and simmer until sauce thickens.
4. Keep ducks warm. Remove fat from baking dish, leaving juices in the bottom. Place dish over moderate heat, stir in port and simmer until reduced by half. Strain juices into orange sauce, bring to simmering and stir in liqueur. Season to taste, add butter and stir until melted.
5. Cut birds into serving portions, arrange on plates and glaze with some of the sauce. Serve remaining sauce separately.

....
Serves 8

tip from the chef

Accompany with saffron rice served into hollow orange rind halves and sprinkled with toasted slivered almonds.

turkey
with apricot seasoning

■ ■ □ | Cooking time: 130 minutes - Preparation time: 15 minutes

method

1. To make seasoning, mix all ingredients, add salt and pepper to taste. Carefully loosen skin over breast of turkey, lay bacon slices under skin. Fill cavity with seasoning. Tie legs together with string, brush with melted butter.

2. Place turkey on a rack in a baking dish, add 1 cup water. Bake in moderate oven for 2 hours or until tender; cover breast and legs with foil after 1 hour to prevent skin burning. Remove turkey from dish, keep warm.

3. To make sauce, drain all but 2 tablespoons of fat from dish, add flour, stir until light brown. Gradually stir in stock, jelly and port, season to taste. Stir until sauce boils and thickens, strain, serve with turkey.

Serves 8

ingredients

> **4 kg/8 lb turkey**
> **3 bacon rashers, halved**
> **30 g/1 oz butter, melted**

seasoning

> **2 cups fresh breadcrumbs**
> **1/4 cup chopped dried apricots**
> **2 cloves garlic, crushed**
> **4 spring onions chopped**
> **2 sticks celery, finely chopped**
> **2 teaspoons green peppercorns, drained and crushed**
> **1 egg, lightly beaten**
> **30 g/1 oz butter, melted**
> **1/4 cup chopped parsley**
> **1 teaspoon dried mixed herbs**

sauce

> **1/4 cup plain flour**
> **2 1/2 cups turkey stock**
> **1 tablespoon redcurrant jelly**
> **2 tablespoons port**
> **salt and freshly ground black pepper**

tip from the chef

As a side dish, glaze some baby onions and carrots.

béarnaise
roast beef

■■□ | Cooking time: 45 minutes - Preparation time: 20 minutes

ingredients

> 1 kg/2 lb beef eye fillet, trimmed of fat
> 1 tablespoon cracked black peppercorns
> 2 teaspoons ground cardamom
> 2 cloves garlic, crushed
> 2 tablespoons oil

béarnaise sauce

> 1¹/2 tablespoons tarragon vinegar
> 1¹/2 tablespoons lemon juice
> 5 egg yolks
> 250 g/¹/2 lb butter

stuffed potatoes

> 8 potatoes, cooked
> ¹/2 cup sour cream
> 4 spring onions, finely chopped
> 1 teaspoon ground cumin
> ¹/4 cup grated mature Cheddar cheese

method

1. Tie beef with string to hold it in shape during cooking. Roll in combined pepper, cardamom and garlic (a).
2. Heat oil in a baking dish, add beef, bake in hot oven for 20 minutes or until cooked as desired, turning beef occasionally. Allow to cool, serve sliced with Béarnaise sauce and stuffed potatoes.
3. To make Béarnaise sauce, simmer vinegar and lemon juice in a small saucepan until reduced to 2 tablespoons, cool. Blend or process egg yolks and vinegar mixture until frothy. With motor running gradually drizzle in hot melted butter (b). Stand, covered, at room temperature.
4. To make stuffed potatoes, cut top from potatoes, reserve. Scoop flesh from center, mash well with a fork, stir in sour cream, spring onions, cumin and cheese. Spoon back into potatoes (c), replace lids. Bake in moderate oven for 20 minutes or until heated through.

....
Serves 8

a

b

c

roast beef
with nut stuffing

■ ■ ■ | Cooking time: 70 minutes - Preparation time: 20 minutes

method

1. To make stuffing, combine all ingredients and be sure mixture is moist, but not wet. Make an incision along beef to form a pocket, cutting only 3/4 of the way through. Fill pocket with stuffing and tie beef with string at 5 cm/2 in intervals.

2. Scatter carrot, celery and onion in the base of a baking dish and dot with butter. Place beef on top of vegetables. Roast in a preheated hot oven for 50-60 minutes, turning beef halfway through cooking time. Remove beef to a serving platter and cover loosely with foil, stand for about 15 minutes before carving.

3. Strain pan juices through a colander into a saucepan, pressing down on vegetables. Add stock and port and bring to the boil. Boil rapidly until liquid is lightly reduced to thin gravy consistency. Season to taste with salt and pepper.

4. Remove strings from beef. Arrange on a heated platter and spoon a little gravy over the top. Garnish platter with watercress. Carve beef into thick slices and serve remaining gravy separately in a heated sauce boat.

ingredients

- > 1 1/2 kg/3 lb beef eye fillet, trimmed of fat
- > 1 large carrot, coarsely chopped
- > 3 sticks celery, coarsely chopped
- > 1 large onion, coarsely chopped
- > 2 tablespoons butter
- > 1 cup beef stock
- > 1/2 cup port

stuffing

- > 1/3 cup coarsely chopped pecans
- > 2 tablespoons butter, melted
- > 2 tablespoons chopped fresh parsley
- > 2 tablespoons honey
- > 1 tablespoon grated orange rind
- > 1/4 cup port
- > 1 egg, beaten
- > salt and freshly ground pepper
- > 2 cups fresh breadcrumbs

Serves 8-10

tip from the chef

If you wish, add 1 tablespoon Dijon mustard to the sauce.

honey-glazed
ham

tropical
glazed ham

■ ■ □ | Cooking time: 45 minutes - Preparation time: 15 minutes

method

1. To remove the rind from ham and score the fat in a diamond pattern, proceed as explained in page 35.
2. To make glaze, combine pineapple juice, Worcestershire sauce, jam, honey, sugar and chutney. Place ham in a large baking dish, brush with glaze. Decorate with cloves and halved cherries.
3. Bake in moderate oven for 45 minutes or until warmed through, brushing occasionally with glaze. Serve sliced.

Serves 8

ingredients

> 1 x 4 kg/8 lb cooked leg of ham
> whole cloves
> glacé cherries

tropical glaze

> 1/4 cup pineapple juice
> 2 teaspoons Worcestershire sauce
> 2 tablespoons apricot jam
> 1 tablespoon honey
> 1/4 cup brown sugar
> 1 tablespoon mango chutney

tip from the chef

A great idea for entertaining a crowd consists in offering mini-sandwiches made out of flavored tiny rolls and slices of this appetizing ham.

barbecued
leg of lamb

■ ■ □ | Cooking time: 25 minutes - Preparation time: 10 minutes

method

1. Lay lamb out flat and season well with black pepper. Place in a shallow glass or ceramic dish.
2. To make marinade, place garlic, oil, lemon juice, marjoram and thyme in a small bowl and mix to combine. Pour marinade over lamb, cover and allow to marinate at room temperature for 3-4 hours, or overnight in the refrigerator.
3. Preheat barbecue to a medium heat. Remove lamb from marinade and reserve marinade. Cook lamb on lightly oiled barbecue grill, turning several times during cooking and basting with reserve marinade, for 15-25 minutes or until cooked to your liking.

ingredients

> 1 1/2-2 kg/3-4 lb leg of lamb, butterflied
> freshly ground black pepper

lemon herb marinade

> 2 cloves garlic, crushed
> 1/4 cup/60 ml/2 fl oz olive oil
> 1/4 cup/60 ml/2 fl oz lemon juice
> 1 tablespoon finely chopped fresh marjoram, or 1 teaspoon dried marjoram
> 1 tablespoon finely chopped fresh thyme, or 1 teaspoon dried thyme

Serves 6

tip from the chef

Your butcher will butterfly the leg of lamb in minutes for you, so you can save precious time.

crusted
pumped leg of lamb

a

■ ■ □ | Cooking time: 150 minutes - Preparation time: 20 minutes

method

1. Place lamb in a large saucepan, add parsley stalks, bay leaf, peppercorns, allspice, vinegar and brown sugar. Add cold water to cover (a). Bring slowly to the boil, cover and simmer for 2 hours or until lamb is tender when pierced with a skewer.

2. Remove saucepan from heat and allow lamb to cool in the cooking liquid. When cold, remove and pat dry with paper towels (b).

3. Mix together breadcrumbs, onion, mint, herbs, salt, pepper, pineapple and beaten egg. Place lamb on a rack in a baking dish, brush with melted butter and press crumb mixture on firmly (c).

4. Bake in a moderately hot oven for 20-25 minutes or until crumbs are crisp and golden. Transfer lamb to a heated platter.

5. Cut limes in half and scoop out pulp (reserve for another use). Fill lime halves with mint jelly and arrange on platter.

ingredients

> 2¼ kg/4½ lb pumped leg of lamb
> parsley stalks
> 1 bay leaf
> 1 teaspoon black peppercorns
> 1 teaspoon whole allspice
> 1 tablespoon vinegar
> 1 tablespoon brown sugar
> 3 cups fresh breadcrumbs
> 1 small onion, grated
> 2 tablespoons chopped fresh mint
> 1 teaspoon mixed dried herbs
> salt and pepper to taste
> ½ cup crushed pineapple
> 1 egg, beaten
> 2 tablespoons butter, melted
> limes and mint jelly to serve

....

Serves 6-8

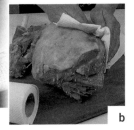

b

c

tip from the chef

This lamb leg, ideal for Easter, results even tastier if brandy or whisky is injected before baking.

lamb with
roasted garlic sauce

■■■ | Cooking time: 130 minutes - Preparation time: 30 minutes

ingredients

> **1 head garlic, cloves separated and peeled**
> **4 canned anchovy fillets, drained**
> **olive oil**
> **freshly ground black pepper**
> **2 kg/4 lb leg of lamb, trimmed of excess fat**
> **1 onion, finely chopped**
> **1 carrot, finely chopped**
> **2 stalks celery, finely chopped**
> **1/2 cup/125 ml/4 fl oz dry white wine**
> **1 cup/250 ml/8 fl oz chicken stock**
> **2 tablespoons chopped fresh parsley**

method

1. Place 4 cloves garlic, anchovy fillets, 1 teaspoon oil and black pepper to taste in a food processor or blender and process to make a smooth paste.
2. Using a sharp knife make several slits in the lamb. Push a little paste into each slit, then rub remaining paste over surface of lamb. Set aside to marinate for 20-30 minutes or in the refrigerator overnight.
3. Place onion, carrot, celery, wine and remaining garlic in a frying pan and cook, stirring, for 5 minutes.
4. Place lamb in a baking dish. Pour wine mixture into dish and bake at 180°C/350°F/Gas 4, adding more wine to keep vegetables moist if necessary, for 1 1/2-2 hours or until lamb is cooked to your liking. Transfer lamb to a large serving platter and keep warm.
5. Skim fat from cooking juices in baking dish. Place juices with vegetables and garlic in a food processor or blender and process until smooth. Transfer mixture to a small saucepan, stir in stock and bring to the boil over a medium heat, reduce heat and simmer for 5 minutes or until sauce reduces and thickens and coats the back of a spoon. Stir in parsley and season to taste with black pepper. To serve, carve lamb and accompany with sauce.

tip from the chef

While this recipe uses a lot of garlic you will find that roasted garlic has a subtle and sweet flavor.

....
Serves 6

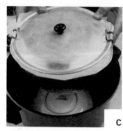

traditional
christmas pudding

■ ■ ■ | Cooking time: 3 hours - Preparation time: 30 minutes

method

1. Place fruits in a large bowl, snipping dates or figs into small pieces (a). Drizzle with brandy or rum, cover and soak overnight.
2. Cream butter, grated citrus rind and brown sugar until light and fluffy. Gradually add beaten eggs, beating well after each addition.
3. Sift together flour, spice, ginger, bicarbonate and salt, add chopped almonds. Stir into creamed mixture alternately with soaked fruit. Stir in breadcrumbs and mix well.
4. Spoon mixture into a lightly greased 7-8 cup pudding basin, smooth the top (b). Cover with a snap-on lid or a double thickness of greaseproof paper tied on with string.
5. Place basin on an old saucer, rounded-side up, in large saucepan (c). Pour boiling water to come halfway up the sides of basin and place over heat. When water returns to the boil, cover saucepan with a lid. Steam pudding for 3 hours, adding boiling water as necessary.
6. Remove basin from water and allow pudding to cool. Cover basin with foil and store in the refrigerator until required. Before serving, steam pudding for a further hour. Turn out onto a heated plate.

ingredients

> 250 g/8 oz each raisins, currants and sultanas
> 60g/2 oz dates or dried figs
> 3 tablespoons brandy or dark rum
> 250 g/8 oz butter, softened
> grated rind of 1 orange and 1 lemon
> 1 cup brown sugar, lightly packed
> 4 eggs, beaten
> 1 cup plain flour
> 1 teaspoon mixed spice
> 1/2 teaspoon ground ginger
> 1/2 teaspoon bicarbonate of soda
> 1/2 teaspoon salt
> 60 g/2 oz blanched almonds, roughly chopped
> 2 cups fresh breadcrumbs

Serves 6-8

tip from the chef

To flame the pudding, warm a little rum or brandy in a small saucepan, set alight and pour over pudding at the table.

simple
christmas pudding

■□□ | Cooking time: 2 hours - Preparation time: 20 minutes

ingredients
> **125 g/4 oz butter**
> **1/2 cup brown sugar, firmly packed**
> **2 eggs**
> **1 1/2 cups self-raising flour**
> **1 teaspoon mixed spice**
> **pinch of salt**
> **1 cup mixed dried fruit**
> **1/2 cup chopped dates**
> **1/4 cup glacé cherries, halved**
> **4 tablespoons sherry or orange juice**
> **sauce of your choice**

method
1. Cream butter and sugar until light and fluffy. Add eggs and beat well (a). Sift flour with spice and salt. Stir into creamed mixture (b). Add mixed fruit (c), dates, cherries and sherry or orange juice and mix well.
2. Spoon mixture into greased 4-cups capacity pudding basin, smooth the top and cover with a tight-fitting lid or a double thickness of greaseproof paper tied securely with string.
3. Place basin in a saucepan on an upturned plate and add enough boiling water to come halfway up the sides of the basin. Cover saucepan and steam pudding briskly for 2 hours, adding extra boiling water as necessary. Turn out pudding onto a heated serving plate and serve with your favorite sauce.

tip from the chef
For the pudding to be lighter, replace the butter for low fat cream cheese.

Serves 6

a

b

c

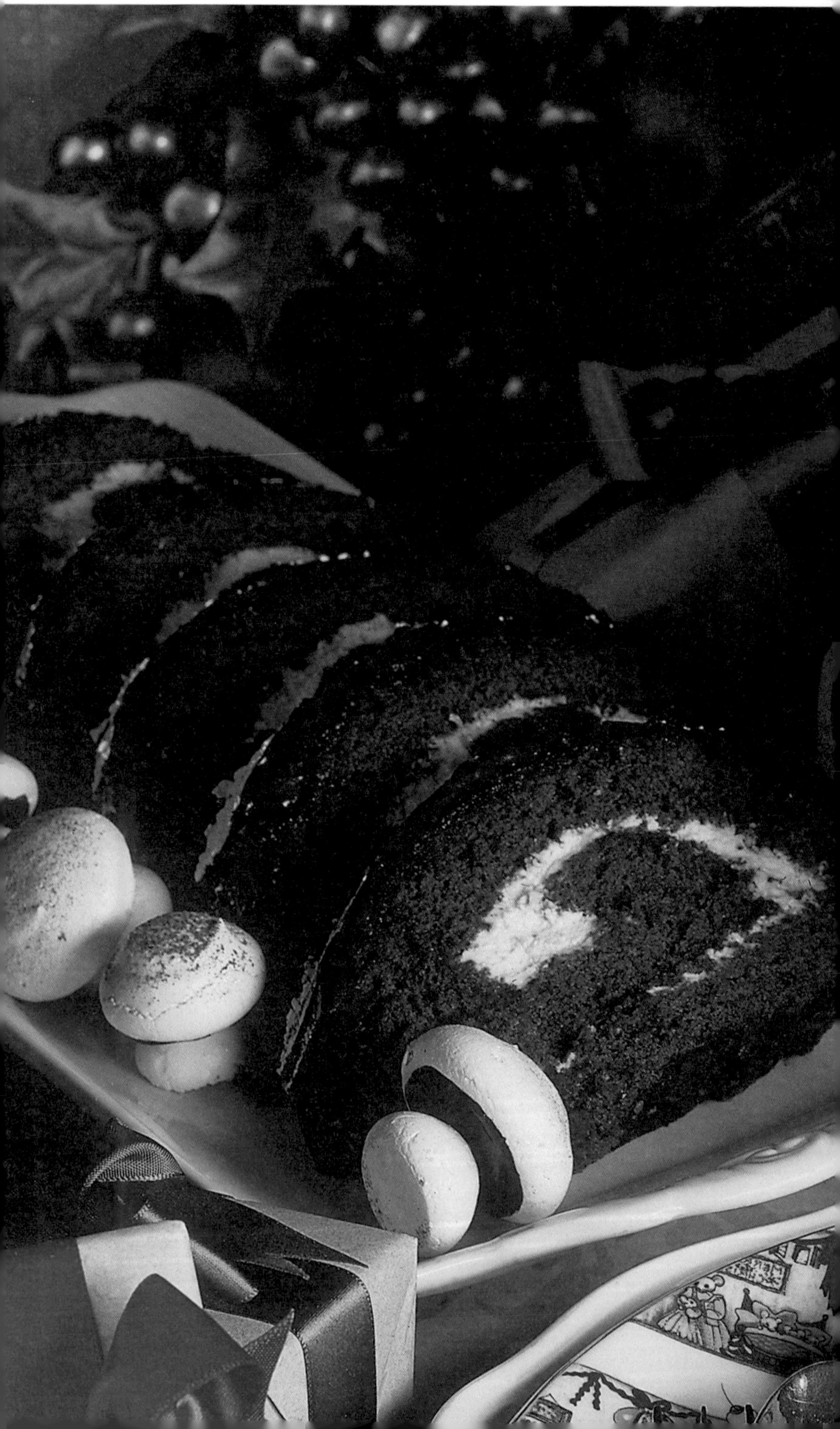

christmas log

■■□ | Cooking time: 35 minutes - Preparation time: 15 minutes

method

1. To make filling, beat ingredients together until soft peaks form. Cover and chill.
2. To make icing, place all ingredients in a saucepan and stir over low heat until well combined. Cool until mixture is almost set. Beat until thick, then chill.
3. To make mushrooms, beat egg white and vinegar until soft peaks form. Gradually add sugar, continue beating until meringue is thick and glossy. Fold in cornflour. Spoon mixture into a piping bag fitted with a plain nozzle and, onto a greased and lined baking tray, pipe button shapes for the tops of mushrooms and small knobs for the stems. Bake at 120°C/250°F/Gas 1/2 for 30 minutes or until meringue is crisp and dry. Allow to cool on tray, then join tops and stems with a little melted chocolate. Sprinkle with cocoa powder.
4. To assemble log, spread cake with filling and roll up. Spread log with icing and mark with a spatula to show textured bark. Decorate with mushrooms and dust with icing sugar.

ingredients

> **26 x 32 cm/10¹/₂ x 12³/₄ in chocolate Swiss roll cake**

rum filling

> ³/₄ cup/185 ml/6 fl oz cream
> 1 tablespoon icing sugar
> 1 tablespoon dark rum

ganache icing

> 185 g/6 oz dark chocolate
> ²/₃ cup/170 ml/5¹/₂ fl oz cream
> 30 g/1 oz butter

meringue mushrooms

> 1 egg white
> ¹/₂ teaspoon vinegar
> ¹/₃ cup/75 g/2¹/₂ oz caster sugar
> 1 teaspoon cornflour
> 30 g/1 oz dark chocolate, melted
> 1 teaspoon cocoa powder

Serves 10

tip from the chef

If you wish, add ¹/₂ cup glacé cherries to the filling.

croquembouche

■□□ | Cooking time: 10 minutes - Preparation time: 15 minutes

ingredients

> **30 profiteroles**

custard filling
> **4 egg yolks**
> **1/2 cup/100 g/3 1/2 oz sugar**
> **1/2 cup/60 g/2 oz flour, sifted**
> **2 1/2 cups/600 ml/1 pt milk**
> **2 tablespoons orange-flavored liqueur**

toffee
> **2 1/2 cups/600 ml/1 pt water**
> **5 cups/1.250 kg/2 1/2 lb sugar**

tip from the chef

To spin toffee, coat the back of two wooden spoons with toffee, place them back to back and gently pull apart. As a thread of toffee is formed continue bringing spoons together and pulling apart until toffee starts to set. Repeat to use all the toffee.

method

1. To make filling, beat egg yolks and sugar until thick and creamy. Fold in flour and 1 tablespoon milk. Scald remaining milk, stir a little into egg mixture, then gradually stir egg mixture into milk. Cook mixture over a low heat, stirring constantly, for 5 minutes or until mixture thickens; cool slightly. Stir in liqueur and set aside to cool completely. Spoon filling into a piping bag fitted with a plain nozzle and pipe a little into each profiterol.

2. To make toffee, place half the water and half the sugar in a heavy-based saucepan and cook over a low heat, stirring constantly, until sugar dissolves. Bring to the boil and boil until golden.

3. To assemble, place a croquembouche cone on a large serving plate. Dip the base of each profiterol in toffee and arrange in layers around the cone. Use remaining water and sugar to make a second quantity of toffee, cool slightly. Spin toffee over and around croquembouche. Stand in a cool place until required. Serve within 6 hours or toffee will soften.

....
Serves 10

rich
fruit cake

a

b

c

■ ■ □ | Cooking time: 3¹/2 hours - Preparation time: 20 minutes

method

1. Place fruit in a bowl, snipping cherries, pineapple and dates into small pieces (a). Toss fruit with brandy. Cover and soak for several days.
2. Grease a 20 cm/8 in round tin. Line the sides with a strip and the base with a circle of brown paper (b). Repeat, using greased greaseproof paper.
3. Beat butter until soft and creamy. Add sugar and beat until dissolved, about 5 minutes. Add eggs one at a time, beating after each addition. Stir in chocolate, essences, glycerin, jam and lemon rind and juice. Sift together flour, spice, ginger and salt, add to butter mixture alternately with soaked fruit, ending with flour. Mix well.
4. Spoon mixture into prepared tin. Lift tin and allow to drop on a flat surface (c) to break up any air bubbles. Bake in a preheated slow oven for 3-3¹/2 hours or until cake is cooked when tested with a skewer.
5. Drizzle cake with extra brandy. Cool on a wire rack, then turn out of tin. Leave paper on cake, wrap in 2 thicknesses of foil and store in an airtight container. Before serving, unwrap cake, brush top with warmed jam and decorate with nuts and cherries.

Makes one 20 cm/8 in cake

ingredients

> **250 g/8 oz each sultanas, currants and raisins**
> **125 g/4 oz mixed peel**
> **250 g/8 oz glacé cherries**
> **60 g/2 oz glacé pineapple**
> **60 g/2 oz dates**
> **6 tablespoons brandy**
> **250 g/8 oz butter, softened**
> **1 cup brown sugar, firmly packed**
> **5 eggs**
> **60 g/2 oz dark chocolate, melted**
> **1 teaspoon each vanilla and almond essences**
> **2 teaspoons glycerin**
> **2 tablespoons raspberry jam**
> **finely grated rind and juice of 1 lemon**
> **2 cups plain flour**
> **1 teaspoon each mixed spice and ground ginger**
> **¹/4 teaspoon salt**

tip from the chef

This cake is ideal to be prepared ahead of time and be stored in the freezer, wrapped as explained at step 5.

quick
fruit cake

■ □ □ | Cooking time: 70 minutes - Preparation time: 15 minutes

ingredients
> **1 kg/2 lb mixed dried fruit**
> **250 g/ 1/2 lb dates,** chopped
> **125 g/4 oz butter**
> **3/4 cup brown sugar**
> **1 teaspoon ground cinnamon**
> **1/2 cup water**
> **1/2 cup brandy**
> **2 eggs, lightly beaten**
> **1 cup self-raising flour**
> **1 cup plain flour**
> glacé cherries for decoration
> blanched almonds for decoration

method
1. Combine mixed fruit, dates, butter, sugar, cinnamon and water in a large saucepan. Stir over heat until butter has melted. Bring to the boil, reduce heat, cook for 3 minutes, cool to room temperature.
2. Stir in brandy and eggs, mix well. Add sifted flours, stir until combined.
3. Spread 1/3 of the mixture into a greased and lined 7 x 25 cm/2 3/4 x 10 in bar pan. Bake in slow oven for 1 hour or until cooked through. Turn out, wrap in a clean tea-towel to cool. Repeat with remaining mixture to make 3 cakes. Decorate with cherries and almonds.

....
Makes 3

tip from the chef
Both brandy and water can be replaced for black beer.

cassata
alla siciliana

■ □ □ I Cooking time: 5 minutes - Preparation time: 10 minutes

method

1. To make filling, place sugar and water in a saucepan and stir over a low heat until sugar dissolves; set aside to cool. Process ricotta cheese until smooth. Transfer to a bowl and mix in syrup and remaining ingredients.
2. Line an 11 x 21 cm/4^{1}/$_{2}$ x 8^{1}/$_{2}$ in loaf tin with plastic food wrap. Cut cake into slices and sprinkle with brandy. Line base and sides of prepared tin with cake. Spoon filling into tin and top with a final layer of cake. Cover and freeze until solid.
3. To make topping, place chocolate and butter in a heatproof bowl over a saucepan of simmering water and stir until melted and well blended. Allow to cool slightly.
4. Turn cassata onto a wire rack and cover with topping. Return to freezer until chocolate sets.

....

Serves 10

ingredients

> 26 x 32 cm/10^{1}/$_{2}$ x 12^{3}/$_{4}$ in Swiss roll cake
> ^{1}/$_{3}$ cup/90 ml/3 fl oz brandy

cassata filling

> ^{1}/$_{2}$ cup/125 g/4 oz sugar
> 2 tablespoons water
> 375 g/12 oz ricotta cheese
> ^{1}/$_{2}$ cup/125 ml/4 fl oz cream, whipped
> 60 g/2 oz mixed peel, chopped
> 100 g/3^{1}/$_{2}$ oz dark chocolate, finely chopped
> 60 g/2 oz glacé cherries, quartered
> 45 g/1^{1}/$_{2}$ oz pistachios, chopped

chocolate topping

> 315 g/10 oz dark chocolate
> 90 g/3 oz butter

tip from the chef

In its homeland, this classic Italian dessert is seen on the Easter Table.

spicy pumpkin pie

■□□ I Cooking time: 50 minutes - Preparation time: 15 minutes

ingredients

pastry

> 1 cup/125 g/4 oz flour
> 1/2 teaspoon baking powder
> 100 g/3¹/² oz butter, cut into pieces
> 1¹/² tablespoons caster sugar
> 1 egg yolk
> 1/2 -1 tablespoon water

spicy pumpkin filling

> 280 g/8 oz pumpkin, cooked and puréed
> 2 eggs, lightly beaten
> 1/2 cup/125 g/4 oz sour cream
> 1/2 cup/125 ml/4 fl oz double cream
> 1/4 cup/90 g/3 oz golden syrup
> 1/2 teaspoon ground nutmeg
> 1/2 teaspoon ground mixed spice
> 1/2 teaspoon ground cinnamon

method

1. To make pastry, process flour and baking powder with butter, until mixture resembles coarse breadcrumbs. Add sugar, egg yolk (a) and enough water to mix to a firm dough. Turn onto a floured surface and knead lightly until smooth. Wrap in plastic food wrap and refrigerate for 30 minutes.

2. To make filling, place all ingredients in a mixing bowl and beat until smooth and well combined (b).

3. Roll pastry out and line a greased 23 cm/9 in flan tin with removable base. Spoon filling into pastry case (c). Bake at 200°C/400°F/Gas 6 for 20 minutes then reduce heat to 160°C/325°F/Gas 3 and bake for 25-30 minutes longer or until filling is set and pastry golden. Allow to stand in tin for 5 minutes before removing. Serve hot, warm or cold with whipped cream.

....
Serves 8

tip from the chef

This pie is perfect for Thanksgiving.
If you wish to give a different presentation, let it cool down, cover with meringue and golden the top under the grill.

a

b

golden
waffles

■□□ | Cooking time: 10 minutes - Preparation time: 10 minutes

method

1. Sift plain flour, self-raising flour, baking powder and salt together into a bowl. Stir in sugar.
2. Whisk together milk, egg yolks and butter. Make a well in the center of flour mixture and mix in milk mixture until just combined.
3. Place egg whites in a bowl and beat until stiff peaks form, then fold into batter.
4. Cook batter in a preheated, greased waffle iron following the manufacturer's instructions. Serve waffles hot with topping of your choice.

Makes about 10 waffles

ingredients

> **2 cups/250 g/8 oz plain flour**
> **1 cup/125 g/4 oz self-raising flour**
> **1 1/2 teaspoons baking powder**
> **1 teaspoon salt**
> **1/4 cup/60 g/2 oz sugar**
> **2 1/4 cups/560 ml/ 18 fl oz milk**
> **3 eggs, separated**
> **120 g/4 oz butter, melted**

tip from the chef

Classic heart-shaped waffles become a perfect dessert for Saint Valentine's Day if served with a scoop of ice-cream and some raspberry compote.

index